YOU HELP YOU

By

Clive Henry

Disclaimer

Clive Henry is not a medical doctor, and is Not liable for risks or issues associated with using or acting upon the information in this book.

The information provided in this book is for educational purposes only, and does not substitute for professional medical advice.

Dedication

This book is dedicated to people that want to improve their health and well-being with simple but effective techniques to help them achieve their goals.

Introduction

Your diet is not only what you eat. It's what you watch, what you listen to, what you read, and the people you hang around.

Be mindful of the things you put into your body - emotionally, spiritually, and physically.

Mind Over Matter

At college I studied Sports Science. It was a study of mind and body from an athlete's perspective. I was a skinny kid that could eat everything, so never had to worry about my weight. Plus, I was hyperactive. Always on the go. As I got older, I did fill out, but my weight has always remained constant. The only time where I remember putting on 30 pounds was when I worked at a sales job in London and was eating fast food at night just before going to bed. My clothes got tight. My year of good living was detrimental to my health.

After getting my yearly doctors check-up I was told my blood pressure was higher than normal, so I made the adjustments to eat healthier and lose the additional weight. It was always shocking to me that gyms didn't stress how important the diet affected your physical well-being. Studies show 80 percent is diet and 20 percent is physical exercise. This book will show a simple but effective method to make positive changes to your health and well-being.

To change your body, you must first change your mind.

You have to decide that you're going to dedicate yourself to do these small changes to really change your world.

Everything in this world requires effort. In the western world we look at film and pop stars and want to emulate what they look like. However, they are a brand and have a team of people from chefs to personal trainers to make sure they stay in optimum shape. They get depressed too, so don't think that they're not human like yourself.

I remember my first time in New York in 1991. It was a culture shock. I saw people from very thin to very large. Both types of people happy and working their jelly, as Beyonce would say. They were comfortable in their own skin. Perception is reality. You have to love you and know that you are what you are; regardless. We are not robots, or one size fits all people.

Depending on where you are in the world a so-called fat person is respected in certain parts of the world. This is their culture. So don't beat yourself up about your weight.

In relationships the shell fades after time and the character shines though.

I want you to get your old photographs out of when you were a child or happy. Put those on your mirror or wall to raise your consciousness. Your state of mind is the major force in how you make decisions.

How The Body Works

The human body is an amazing organic machine that is self-healing and self-regulating to give you the best performance to prolong your life. Most tasks the body performs are automatic. You don't need to think for your heart to beat. However, you do need to think to eat food.

There are many people that use the gym, but how many people are advised with the diet and really understand how the body works?

I have heard shocking conversations that think that 30 minutes in the gym can eliminate the 1000 calorie meal that a person has just eaten.

So many people go to the gym to lose weight or tone their bodies, but end up gaining weight because they don't understand how the body works.

Hopefully, this book will help you to get a better understanding of putting theory to practice and getting the most out of your diet.

In the UK the daily calorie intake for men is 2500 and for women it is 2000. This is only a guide as people are different in height and weight and also body type.

Tools For the Job

1 bathroom scale, 1 diary, refuse bags or cling film, and incense sticks (Frankincense, Sage, or Cobalt).

The body is an organic machine that works to sustain your life. The food and drink you consume is used as energy to fuel your body. The waste your body doesn't need is disposed of when you go to the toilet. Before you start you need to have an idea of where you're at with your fitness, so you can improve.

Below are the steps that have helped others:

1. Weigh yourself with the bathroom scales
    and record your results in your diary.
    Ideally first thing in the morning. You will
    need to do this each week. Getting this
    feedback will help you improve. You are
    your own science project. Research!

2. For 3 days write down the time, date, and
    everything you eat. Also record how you
    feel that day.

3. With the 3 days that you recorded what you ate, including the times you ate. Now is the time to analyse what types of foods you're eating.

4. Are you eating the majority of Carbohydrates, proteins, fibre or fats? Also visit Google or YouTube for these food types to get a clear understanding of what your diet contains.

After you establish where you need to, adjust your food types.

5. You need to introduce better foods that will help you achieve your goals. I believe in gradual change, so you can form a consistent habit and stay in shape - mentally and physically. What I would advise is to start eating on a 7-inch plate to reduce your portion sizes. The psychology here is a full plate tricks your mind into making you feel full quicker, and in turn will help your stomach shrink.

6. Exercise: I advise you to do 10 - 30 minutes of exercise each day. The more calories you burn the more the body will regulate your weight.

7. Try putting cling film or black bin liners under your clothes while you work out. You will sweat more and lose weight faster. You can put this around your stomach, arms or legs. I advise you to drink plenty of water while you are on this new program. This will aid the flushing out of toxins in the body and stop dehydration.

8. Remember, the body is 70% water, so it's a good thing. Water is also the fluid that will help the body to function at its peak performance.

9. Don't starve yourself. The body is a machine that will slow your metabolism down to save your life. The body doesn't have eyes, so can only assume, "We haven't eaten for a long time. We don't know when we're going to get our next meal. Slow everything down and store it as fat for the future." Eating smaller portions with regular exercise is the common way to success with your diet.

10. You know your body type. Be comfortable in your own skin. If you have curves, you have curves. we are all made uniquely different.

Best of luck!

Food Types

Carbohydrates (sugars and starches) - These are foods where you get fast energy. They are used in the body first and you usually get tired quickly from physical exercise when your body uses this type of energy.

Found in foods like: Breads, grains, fruit, vegetables, milk, beer, wine and sugar snacks.

Broken down into glucose, used to supply energy to cells. Extra is stored in the liver.

Proteins - These foods are used to build muscle and essential body functions.

Found in foods like: Eggs, meat, milk, nuts and seeds.

Broken down into <u>amino acids</u>, used to build muscle and to make other proteins that are essential for the body to function.

Fats - These foods are used to make cell linings and hormones.

Found in foods like: Oils, butter, egg yolks, animal products.

Broken down into fatty acids. Extra is stored in fat cells.

Vitamins and Minerals - Are nutrients your body needs in small doses to work properly and stay healthy. Found in food, but taken by supplements (tablet or liquid form) if you can't get enough from your diet.

Weigh yourself first thing in the morning. Ideally on the same day of each week. Record your weight.

You are your own science experiment. Record your progress. Improve from the feedback.

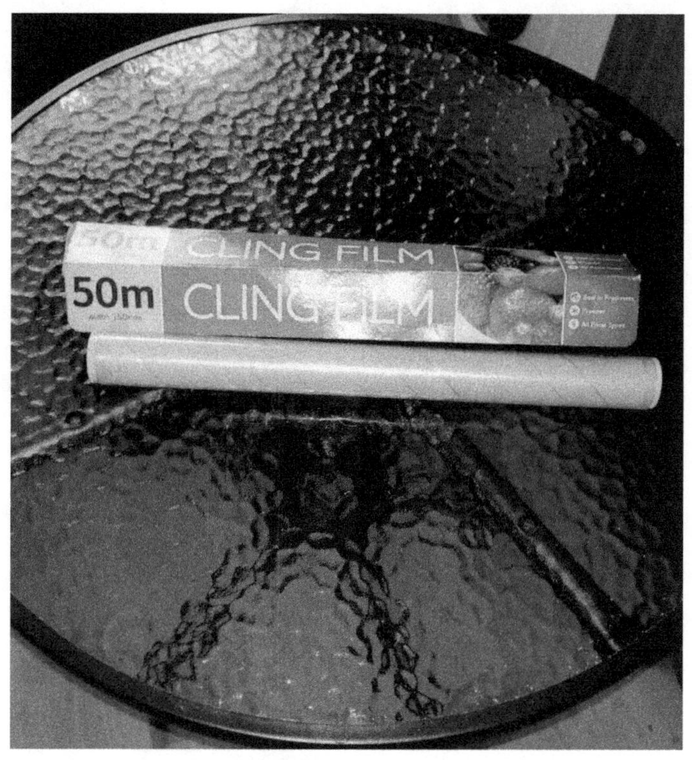

Wrap your body in cling film to help burn calories by sweating to lose weight.

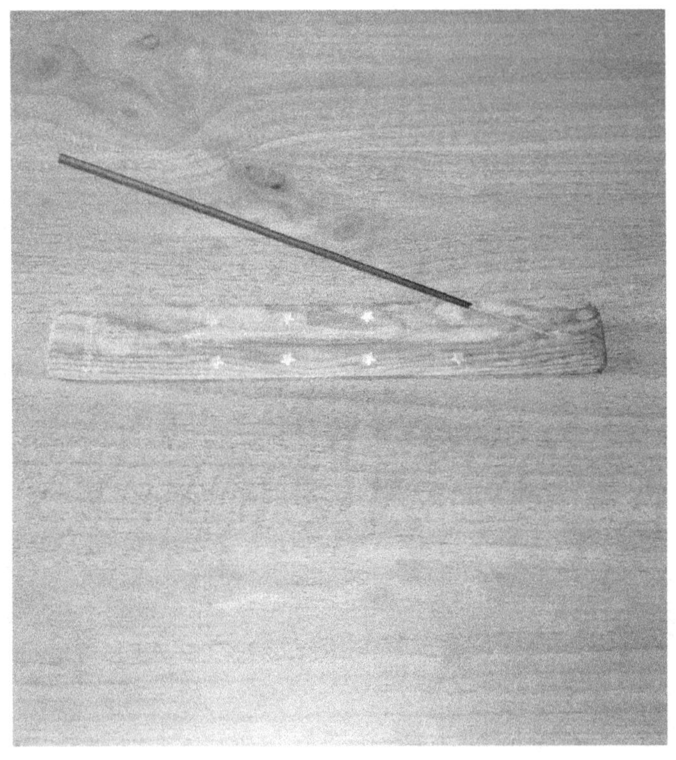

Burn incense like Cobalt, Sage or Frankincense
to lift your mood and remove negative energy.

The body is 70 percent water. Drink plenty of water to flush out toxins in the body and aid body functions.

Help and Support

Changing habits is always a difficult thing. I want you to know you are not alone and I will support you on your journey. For a small lifetime fee of £10.00 I will give you one on one direction via phone, zoom calls or in person if you need this and are willing to pay for my travel. Never be scared to ask for help. We live in a world where people value things over people, but there are still good people out there. I live by the laws of karma and want everyone to have love and light in their lives. Caring is sharing. Cliche - but so very true. Now it's time that You Help You!

Clive Henry

I am the author of You Help You and Racism Is Real: Clive Henry. I want to release books that will help others to achieve their goals or educate people to live in a better world.

My contact details:

Email: cliveh26@gmail.com

Cash App: £clivehenry23

PayPal: cliveh26@gmail.com

Zoom: cliveh26@gmail.com

Twitter: @clivehenry1

Instagram: racismisreal

Yours Truly,

Clive Henry